Contents

My Country

Monday, 2 March

18 Castle Road
Oranmore
County Galway
Ireland

Dear Lou,

Dia duit! (You say 'GEE-a gwitch'. This means 'hello' in Irish.)

My name is Sinéad Walsh (say 'Shin-ade') and I'm 11 years old.
I live in a town called Oranmore in Ireland. I have one brother,
Séamus (say 'Shay-mus'), who is 16. We usually speak English at
home, but we all speak Irish too.

Write soon!

From

Sinéad

Here is my family
outside our house.
I'm the one wearing
the striped
cardigan! ➔

Ireland is an island in north-west Europe. In the past, Ireland was invaded many times. The Celts came in ancient times. The English arrived in the 12th century. The Republic of Ireland became independent from the UK in 1921.

Ireland's place in the world.

ATLANTIC OCEAN

North Channel

NORTHERN IRELAND

Sligo

SLIGO

Shannon

CAVAN

Drogheda

Irish Sea

IRELAND

GALWAY

Galway City • Oranmore

Galway Bay

Cliffs of Moher

Shannon

DUBLIN

WICKLOW MOUNTAINS

Limerick

LIMERICK

Barrow

Suir

Wexford

Waterford

St George's Channel

Carrantuohill △1,041m

Cork

Celtic Sea

N

0   25   50 kilometres
0   25   50 miles

The Republic of Ireland is independent, while Northern Ireland is part of the UK. The Republic of Ireland is known as Ireland or Éire.

Oranmore is a small town on the west coast of Ireland. The town lies on the edge of Oranmore Bay, which is an inlet of Galway Bay.

Around 8,000 people live in Oranmore and the population is increasing. The main industry used to be dairy farming, but tourism and manufacturing are becoming more important. Many people from Oranmore work in Galway City, about 10 km away.

This is the main street in Oranmore. These buildings are in the traditional style, but new housing estates are being built nearby.

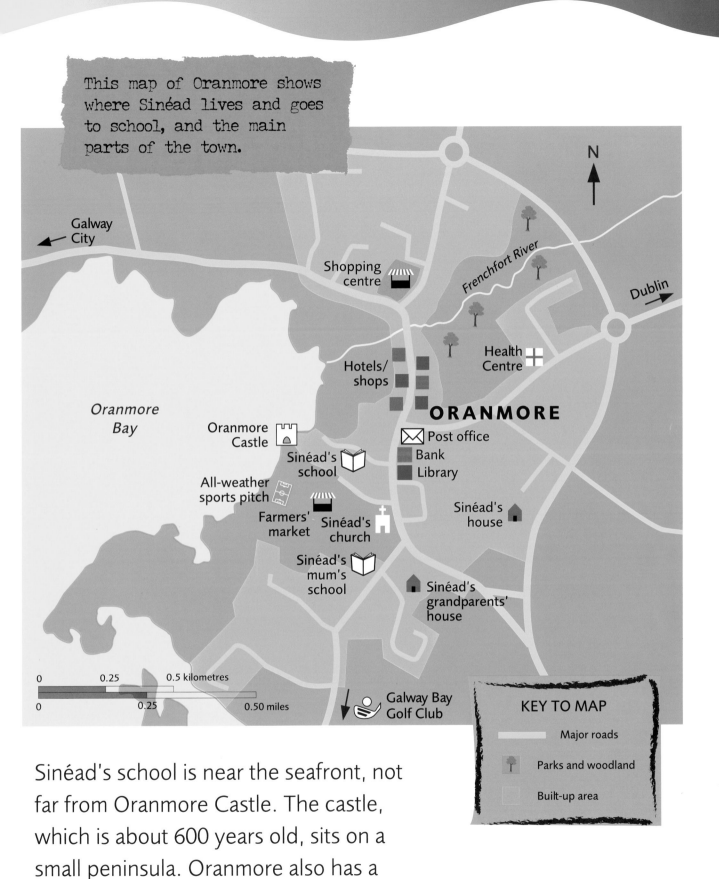

This map of Oranmore shows where Sinéad lives and goes to school, and the main parts of the town.

Galway City

Shopping centre

Frenchfort River

Dublin

N

Hotels/ shops

Health Centre

ORANMORE

Oranmore Bay

Oranmore Castle

Sinéad's school

Post office

Bank

Library

Sinéad's house

All-weather sports pitch

Farmers' market

Sinéad's church

Sinéad's mum's school

Sinéad's grandparents' house

0   0.25   0.5 kilometres

0   0.25   0.50 miles

Galway Bay Golf Club

KEY TO MAP

Major roads

Parks and woodland

Built-up area

Sinéad's school is near the seafront, not far from Oranmore Castle. The castle, which is about 600 years old, sits on a small peninsula. Oranmore also has a shopping centre, a library and a church.

Landscape and Weather

The west coast of Ireland has beautiful scenery and attracts many tourists. There are peninsulas and high cliffs along the coast, and wide beaches too.

Ireland is known as the Emerald Isle because of its beautiful green landscape. Nearly two-thirds of the land is used for farming.

The middle of the country is quite flat. In the east, the coastline slopes gently down towards the sea.

Ireland has a temperate climate. The temperature is rarely hotter than 20°C or below freezing. It is often rainy, especially over high ground.

The dramatic Cliffs of Moher are on the west coast of Ireland.

Oranmore's Climate

January

Temperature

7.2°C

120.8mm

Rainfall

July

Temperature

18.4°C

63.8mm

Rainfall

At Home

Sinéad's home is just outside the centre of Oranmore.
It takes five minutes to get to the town centre by car.
Sinéad's house was built only five years ago.

Sinéad lives in a modern
detached house. The limestone
bricks on the side are
traditional in this area.

Winters in Oranmore can be cold, wet and windy.
The house has central heating, using oil as fuel.

Sinéad is learning to play the piano and the violin. She practises them both nearly every day. Séamus plays the guitar.

The house has a living room, kitchen with a dining area, and a games room. Sinéad and her brother each have their own bedroom.

The house has a large garden — big enough for a giant trampoline and basketball hoops.

Sinéad lays the table for the evening meal. She folds the napkins so they look neat.

Sinéad's mum is from Oranmore, and her parents and other family members live nearby. Sinéad sees her grandparents every couple of days.

In the games room, Sinéad and her brother practise their table-tennis skills. It's the perfect activity for rainy days.

Friday, 3 April

18 Castle Road
Oranmore
County Galway
Ireland

Dia duit Lou!

Did I tell you that my aunt and uncle live on a farm? It's not too far away, so I can visit them often. Uncle Séamus and Auntie Marie have beef cattle. They also have donkeys, cats and dogs. And last week, Sweetie the cattle dog had two puppies. Best of all, I was allowed to name them!

Do you have any pets?

Slán! (You say 'Slawhn' – it means 'goodbye'.)

Sinéad

Here I am with the two new puppies, Bruno and Poppy. When they grow up, they'll help to herd the cattle too.

Food and Mealtimes

On schooldays, Sinéad usually eats cereal, yogurt and toast for breakfast. She drinks fruit juice. At dinnertime, the family enjoys eating pasta or rice, as well as meat dishes, such as steak and potatoes.

At the weekend, Sinéad and her family have French croissants for a breakfast treat!

Few Irish schools provide cooked meals. Sinéad and her friends take a packed lunch to school.

Italian food has become popular in Ireland. Pasta is Sinéad's favourite meal.

Like most Irish families, Sinéad and her family do most of their shopping at a large supermarket. There is one in the Oranmore shopping centre. They buy some food, such as fruit, vegetables and locally caught fish, at the Thursday farmers' market. There is also a farmers' market in Galway City on Saturdays.

Saturday, 2 May

18 Castle Road
Oranmore
County Galway
Ireland

Dia duit Lou!

You asked me for an Irish recipe. Here's how to make Irish brown soda bread.

You will need: 225g wholemeal flour, 225g plain flour, 2 teaspoons bicarbonate of soda, 1 teaspoon salt, 1 tablespoon vegetable oil, 425ml buttermilk (a sour kind of milk).

1. Preheat the oven to 200°C (gas mark 6).
2. Mix the vegetable oil with the buttermilk.
3. Tip the wholemeal flour, plain flour, bicarbonate of soda and salt into a large mixing bowl. Mix them together.

I'm making brown soda bread with my grandmother at her house. Here, we are mixing the dry ingredients together.

I'm trying not to spill any of the buttermilk!

4. Make a well in the middle of the mixture and pour in the oil and buttermilk. Then mix together with a fork until you have a soft dough.

5. Put the dough on to a lightly floured surface, knead for a few seconds and then shape into a round loaf.

6. Place on a greased baking tray and cut a cross on top of the loaf. Cover the loaf tightly with foil.

7. Ask an adult to bake the loaf for 30 minutes – or until it sounds hollow when tapped.

I hope you like it as much as I do!

Slán!

Sinéad

Here's the finished bread. We serve it warm or toasted.

School Day

Sinéad's school day begins at 8.50 a.m. and finishes at 2.30 p.m. There is a lunch break from 12.30–1 p.m. Sinéad goes to a single-sex school, as do nearly half of all children in Ireland.

This is Sinéad's grandfather picking her up after school. Her mum drives her to school in the morning.

There are three terms, with short holidays at Christmas and Easter. The summer holidays in July and August are eight weeks long.

Irish is Sinéad's favourite subject. Here, she reads out Irish words in class.

Lessons at Sinéad's school are usually taught in English, but the teachers speak Irish to the students outside lessons. In some schools in Ireland, Irish is the only language spoken.

Sinéad does a science experiment with her friends Aisling and Janessa.

At Sinéad's school, the girls learn Irish dancing in PE.

At breaktime, from 10.50 to 11.00 a.m., Sinéad and her friends play games such as hopscotch, sing traditional rhymes or chat. After school, Sinéad goes to Irish dancing and ballet, and plays camogie.

Sinéad's class usually says prayers at the beginning and end of every school day. Religious education is important in Irish schools.

Friday, 5 June

18 Castle Road
Oranmore
County Galway
Ireland

Dia duit Lou!

Guess what I've entered into a competition at school...
a potato! We've been growing potatoes in compost bags with
our teacher, Mr Fahy. They grow really well in our climate.
We entered a competition for primary schools all over
Ireland to see who could grow the biggest potato. I hope
our school wins!

Have you ever grown anything?

Slán!

Sinéad

Here are some of the potatoes that
our class grew. If I don't win, Mum's
going to use mine to make mash!

Off to Work

Like many families in Ireland, both of Sinéad's parents work. Her mum is a teacher and her dad is a pharmacist. They both drive to work because no buses come near their home.

Sinéad's mum teaches a drama class. She has asked the pupils to pretend they are cold.

These American tourists are looking at glass bowls. They were made using the traditional Irish skill of glass blowing.

Most Irish people work in industry and services. Industries include mining, food, chemicals, machinery and computer software. Tourism is an important service.

International businesses, especially computer companies, have set up branches in Ireland.

Free Time

Like many Irish people, Sinéad and her family enjoy exploring the local countryside in summer. They prefer the cinema or bowling in the wintertime. At weekends, they often go on day trips to visit relatives. They fly to France for their summer break.

Sinéad practises Gaelic football every week. This Irish sport is a mixture of soccer and rugby.

Surfing is becoming very popular in Ireland among young people. The west coast has some of the best surfing beaches in Europe.

Saturday, 11 July

18 Castle Road
Oranmore
County Galway
Ireland

Dia duit Lou!

People in Ireland love horses, and the countryside is perfect for horse riding. Today, I had a riding lesson at a stable near Galway City. It was brilliant! It's my favourite activity. I love the freedom that I feel when I'm riding.

I'm going to the Galway Races next week. Every year in July my whole family goes for a special treat. I can't wait!

What do you like to do in your spare time?

Slán!

Sinéad

Here I am riding Grey Rosie. She's my favourite pony because she's very clever and so gentle with me.

Religion

Nearly 90 per cent of people in Ireland are Roman Catholics. Many people go to church regularly. Sinéad and her family go to church every Sunday. They celebrate the religious festivals too.

ST.JOSEPH'S HOLY WELL

All over Ireland there are Catholic shrines like this one. They are often close to holy wells — places that are linked to Catholic saints. Many people believe that the water can heal the sick.

Sinéad's mum stands with her class. Her pupils have just received their First Communion, one of the most important ceremonies for Roman Catholics.

In many Irish cities, towns and villages, people celebrate Saint Patrick's Day by taking part in parades and festivals.

The main festivals in Ireland are Christmas, Easter and Saint Patrick's Day. Saint Patrick is one of the patron saints of Ireland and his feast day is held on 17 March. That day is a national holiday in Ireland. It is also celebrated in many countries where Irish people live.

Fact File

Capital city: The capital city of Ireland is Dublin.

Other major cities: Cork, Galway City, Limerick, Waterford.

Size: 70,282km^2.

Population: 4.2 million. This is about half of the population of New York City, in the USA.

Languages: The main language is English, but Irish is taught in all schools.

Main religions: About 87% of the population is Roman Catholic, while 3% belong to the Church of Ireland.

Longest river: The Shannon. The Shannon flows from County Cavan in the north to County Limerick in the south. The river is 386km long.

Highest mountain: Carrantuohill (1,041m).

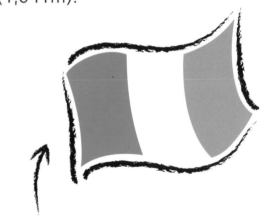

Flag: The Irish flag has wide vertical stripes of green, white and orange.

European Union (EU): Ireland joined the EU in 1973.

Famous Irish people: U2 is a rock band from Dublin that has sold more than 170 million albums worldwide. The lead singer, Bono, is also well known for his charity work. Eoin Colfer has written many bestselling children's books including the *Artemis Fowl* series. Colin Farrell, Jonathan Rhys Meyers and Pierce Brosnan are all famous actors from Ireland. Padraig Harrington is a famous Irish golfer.

Currency: Euro (€), divided into cents (1€ = 100 cent). On one side of the coins, there is an Irish harp and the word Éire, the Irish word for 'Ireland'.

Main industries: Ireland's main industries are steel and lead production, chemicals and pharmaceuticals (drugs and medicines), machinery, computer software and tourism.

Main festivals: Christmas, Easter, St Patrick's Day (17 March).

Stamps: Irish stamps celebrate special events and show famous people, art and nature.

Glossary

camogie A game a little like hockey.

Celts People from western Europe who settled in ancient Britain and Ireland before the Romans came.

climate The normal weather in a place.

detached Standing alone.

Dia duit! This means 'hello' in Irish.

farmers' market A place where locally grown food is sold.

feast day The day on which a Christian celebration is held every year.

harp A stringed musical instrument.

inlet A narrow strip of water that stretches into the land from the sea.

limestone A hard type of rock used as a building material.

manufacturing Making goods in large amounts.

patron saint A special saint of a place or person.

peninsula A long, narrow piece of land that sticks out into the sea.

pharmacist A person who prepares or sells medicines.

Roman Catholic A member of the Roman Catholic Church, the part of the Christian Church that is led by the Pope.

saint A person who the Church sees as very holy because of the way he or she lived or died.

service A business that does something for people but does not make goods.

shrine A place that contains a religious statue or other objects. People pray there.

single-sex school A school attended by boys or girls, but not both.

Slán This means 'goodbye' in Irish.

temperate With mild temperatures – not very hot or very cold.

Further Information

Information books:

The Changing Face of Ireland by Kay Barnham (Wayland, 2005)

The Great Famine by Feargal Brougham and Caroline Farrell (Evans, 2007)

Ireland: In the Children's Own Words by Susie Brooks (Chrysalis Children's Books, 2005)

Step-Up History: Famous Irish Men and Women by Sean Sheehan (Evans 2008)

A Visit to Ireland by Rob Alcroft (Heinemann, 2008)

War and Change: Ireland 1918–1924 by Richard McConnell (Evans, 2007)

Fiction:

Irish Fairy Tales by Joseph Jacobs (Wordsworth Editions, 2001)

Irish Myths and Legends by Ita Daly and Bee Willey (Oxford University Press, 2006)

Stories from Ireland by Ita Daly (Oxford University Press, 2009)

Websites:

Discover Ireland
http://www.discoverireland.ie/
What to do and where to go in Ireland.

Oranmore – Gateway to the West of Ireland
http://www.oranmore.ie/
Oranmore's official website, produced by the Oranmore Community Development Association.

The World Factbook
https://www.cia.gov/library/publications/the-world-factbook/geos/ei.html
Facts and figures about Ireland.

Index